COCKROACHES

John Kirkwood

Grolier
an imprint of

www.scholastic.com/librarypublishing

Published 2009 by Grolier
An Imprint of Scholastic Library Publishing
Old Sherman Turnpike
Danbury, Connecticut 06816

For The Brown Reference Group
Project Editor: Jolyon Goddard
Picture Researchers: Clare Newman, Sophie
Mortimer
Designer: Sarah Williams
Managing Editor: Tim Harris

Volume ISBN-13: 978-0-7172-8061-2
Volume ISBN-10: 0-7172-8061-6

**Library of Congress
Cataloging-in-Publication Data**

Nature's children. Set 6.
    p. cm.
  Includes index.
  ISBN-13: 978-0-7172-8085-8
  ISBN-10: 0-7172-8085-3
  1. Animals--Encyclopedias, Juvenile. 1.
Grolier (Firm)
  QL49.N387 2009
  590.3--dc22
                        2008014675

Printed and bound in China

PICTURE CREDITS

Front Cover: **Shutterstock**: Kurt_G.

Back Cover: **Shutterstock**: Eu Toch, Vincent
Drolet Lamarre, Andre Maritz, Dmitrijs
Mihejevs.

Corbis: Anthony Bannister 25, Daniel
Heuclin 13, Wayne Lawler 30, Richard T.
Nowitz 38, Karen Tweedy Holmes 10;
NHPA: A.N.T. Photo Library 9, Anthony
Bannister 22, 26, 41; G. I. Bernard 14, 34,
Stephen Dalton 6, 37, 46, Martin Harvey
18–19, Brian Hawkes 21, Dr Ivan Polunin
42; **Oxford Scientific Films**: 29, 33,
Scott Camazine and Sue Trainor 46;
Shutterstock: Steve McWilliam 2–3, 5,
Connie Wade 4.

Contents

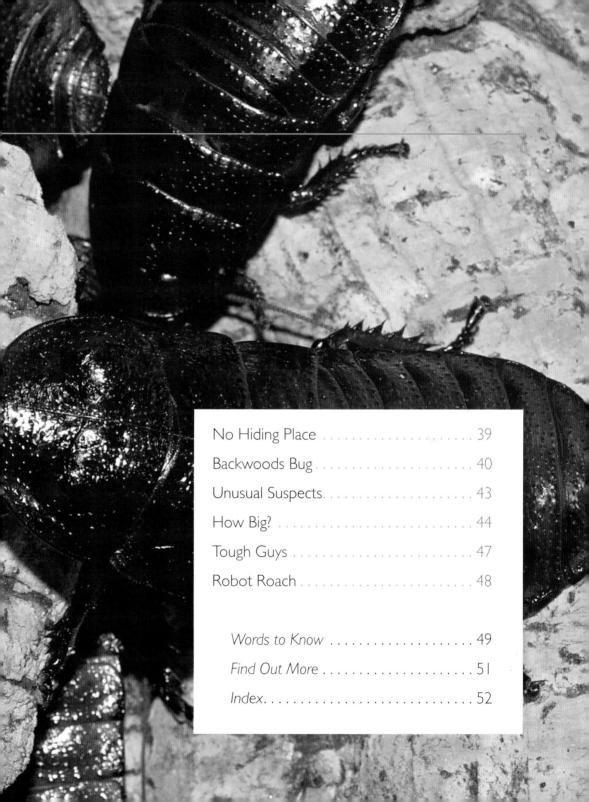

FACT FILE: Cockroaches

Class	Insects (Insecta)
Order	Cockroaches (Blattaria)
Families	There are five families of cockroaches
Genera	Many genera
Species	About 5,000 species
World distribution	All tropical and subtropical regions; can survive in colder climates inside heated buildings
Habitat	Warm, moist, and dark locations
Distinctive physical characteristics	Flattened, oval body; long antennas; shiny black or brown external covering; backward-pointing head and jaws
Habits	Cockroaches lurk in dark, warm, and humid places looking for food; while most cockroaches do not fly, some can run very fast; mainly active at night
Diet	A wide range of plant and animal products

Introduction

Cockroaches are true survivors. They have been on Earth for millions and millions of years and are likely to be around for millions of years to come. Cockroaches can squeeze into narrow cracks, where they rest. These insects emerge at night—often in large groups—using their sharp senses to search for food. They can climb walls with ease and run fast. Scientists have even designed miniature robots based on the cockroach's body plan and how the insect runs.

The word "cockroach" comes from the Spanish word for the the insect, *cucaracha.*

An unwelcome
guest—an American
cockroach climbs the
tiles of a kitchen wall.

Not Just a Pest

Most cockroaches live in the warm, moist regions of the world, such as the tropics. However, just a few **species** of cockroaches live close to people. They live where they can find food easily, such as in kitchens. Cockroaches often hide in dark corners, where food gets spilled, such as behind the stove. The cockroaches that live alongside humans eat our food and do a lot of damage, making dirt and sometimes spreading disease as they move around. They also chew on a wide range of items, including the paper in books and fabrics in clothing. They can be very unwelcome guests in a home.

Although people dislike the cockroaches that live in their homes, not all cockroaches are pests—many species live far away from people. Wherever cockroaches live, these insects have a remarkable ability to withstand harsh conditions and are great survivors.

Cockroach Kingdom

Cockroaches are insects with wings. Compared to many other insects, they are thought to be primitive, or uncomplicated. That means that they have not **adapted** to one lifestyle, **habitat**, or type of food. They are, however, very successful creatures. There are some 5,000 different species of cockroaches. Because they are not suited to just one type of habitat, diet, or lifestyle, they can survive in a wide variety of places and live on many different foods.

Like the body of other insects, a cockroach's body is divided into three parts: the head, **thorax**, and **abdomen**. They also have feelers, or **antennas**, and three pairs of legs attached to the thorax. Male cockroaches usually have two sets of wings. Most cockroaches have legs with three joints. That means they have 18 knees! A cockroach's skeleton is on the outside of its body and is made of a hard substance called **chitin**.

Like other insects, a
cockroach has a tough
outer skeleton. This
cockroach lives in the
deserts of Australia.

9

Watch me go! Many
cockroach species are
wingless and rely on
running speed to
escape enemies.

On the Run

Most species of cockroaches can move incredibly fast for their size. Their speed helps them get away from danger and into hiding quickly. So if you ever see a cockroach scuttling fast across the floor, remember that some cockroaches are record breakers. In fact, certain large tropical cockroaches hold the record for the fastest-moving land insects in the world. In 1991 at the University of California, a cockroach set a record speed of a little more than 3 miles (4.8 km) per hour, or 50 body lengths a second. That is the same as a person running 330 feet (100 m) in a second, ten times faster than the fastest human runner in the world. If you were the size of a cockroach, you would never catch up with one.

Food and Drink

Cockroaches—sometimes called "roaches"—love to eat the same foods as humans. But there are also a lot of other things they like to eat. They have powerful jaws to help them chomp through their food. When roaches chew, their mouth moves from side to side rather than up and down like a human's. Their mouthparts point backward. Most other insects have mouthparts that point either forward or downward. Their sense of smell is partly located in their mouth and partly in their antennas. They also have **salivary glands** in their mouth. Salivary glands produce a fluid that helps them **digest** their food. Salivary glands also allow them to spit—a nasty roach habit.

Cockroaches like regular food supplies. But they can do without food for up to a month. However, they cannot live without water for more than a week. Cockroaches get a lot of the water they need from their food.

A cockroach bites
into a slice of bread.

13

A baby cockroach hides by posing as a dead leaf.

On the Outside

It is not hard to recognize a cockroach. Cockroaches usually have a flattened, oval-shaped shiny brown or black body, long antennas, and a head that tilts downward. You can tell a male from a female because males usually have two pairs of wings, while females either lack wings or have wings that are too small for flying.

Humans and many other animals have a skeleton inside their body. Cockroaches have their skeleton on the outside. This kind of skeleton is called an exoskeleton. It supports their insides and gives protection. Because it is hard, the skeleton cannot grow. Therefore, cockroaches shed their skeleton several times each year and quickly expand before their new skeleton forms. You can tell when a roach has just shed its skeleton because it has white skin. About eight hours after shedding, roaches turn brown or black again.

On the Inside

Inside their outer skeleton, cockroaches have a white substance called the **fat body**. The fat body is a bit like the fat humans have in their body. Like human fat, it stores energy, but cockroach fat also helps with digestion and can make poisons, such as **insecticides**, less harmful.

All of the cockroach's digestive organs are found inside its body. It takes about two days for food to go all the way through a roach's digestive system. After being chewed, the food travels down the throat, or **esophagus**, to the stomach. At the end of the esophagus is the **crop**, where food is stored temporarily. A second set of teeth grinds the food into smaller pieces in a section called the **gizzard**. The food is absorbed into the blood in the **midgut**. Other organs remove any waste.

Heart and Lungs

You will never see a cockroach open its mouth and take a deep breath. That is because cockroaches do not breathe through their mouth. They don't have lungs like us, either. Instead, they breathe through tiny holes, called **spiracles**, in the sides of their body. These holes take in the air they need to live and pass it to all the other parts of the body. A cockroach can survive without breathing for 40 minutes.

A cockroach can also live for some time if its heart stops working. That is because the heart in a cockroach has a far less important role than it does in a human. The heart of a cockroach is only a simple tube. Valves in the tube allow blood to pass along tiny blood vessels to and from the cockroach's body parts. Unlike human blood, a cockroach's blood is white.

18

Cockroaches often
come together in large
groups, or swarms.

Getting Around

If you crept up on a cockroach without it noticing you, the chances are you would see it doing nothing. That is because cockroaches like to spend about three-quarters of their time resting. But when they want to, cockroaches can get around very easily. They are excellent climbers and runners and are good at getting into and through tiny spaces. An adult male pest cockroach can squeeze into a space $\frac{1}{16}$ inch (1.5 mm) wide. A young roach can get into a crack that is almost as thin as a pin.

Walls are not a barrier to roaches because they have tiny claws on their feet that can grip onto almost any surface. One of their favorite ways of getting from place to place in towns and cities is to go along pipes and electricity cables. Cockroaches don't like the cold, so when the temperature drops they often follow hot-water pipes.

This giant cockroach has flown up to the ceiling, which it grips with its tiny claws.

A cockroach sits on a leaf enjoying the warmth of the sun in a forest in South Africa.

Most Like it Hot

Most of the thousands of roach species live in tropical parts of the world. However, different species of roaches are found everywhere in the world, even in very cold places, where you might think they would freeze to death.

The pest species can live in temperatures as low as 32°F (0°C), but will die if it gets much colder. So if the temperature falls below freezing, they survive by moving in with humans. They especially like to live in centrally heated buildings or near sources of heat such as boiler rooms. The heating of buildings in winter has allowed roaches to spread to all the places where humans live.

Roaches cannot survive at very high temperatures, so heat is often used to kill them. Sometimes, an infested house is wrapped in a canvas tent, and air at 140°F (60°C) is blown into the tent for four hours. At the end of this time every part of the house will have heated up to 120°F (50°C) or more—hot enough to kill off all insects, including cockroaches.

Pairing Up

Cockroaches are not romantic creatures. Instead of getting to know each other, cockroaches simply find their partners by sniffing the air! When a female is ready to mate, she gives off a special scent. The odor attracts the male to her, and mating takes place. The attraction of this odor is so strong that people use it to lure some pest cockroaches toward poisoned bait.

During mating, a male fertilizes a female's eggs. That allows the eggs to develop into a new generation of cockroaches.

Two male cockroaches are drawn to the enticing smell of a female.

25

This Cape mountain cockroach is one of the few species that give birth to live babies. Here is a mother with her newborns.

Eggs in One Basket

After the eggs are fertilized by the male, young cockroaches develop inside them—just like the young of other insect species. The eggs are usually glued together by the female to form a packet, or egg case. This packet will contain from 16 to 64 eggs, depending on the species and on how much food the mother can find. Females from one family of cockroaches keep their eggs inside their body and give birth to live young. In the other species of cockroaches, the female carries the egg case with her for a while.

Some species carry the egg case until hatching time is close, while others deposit their egg cases soon after they have been formed. In the common household pest species, such as the German cockroach, the female produces an egg case 72 hours after mating and then carries it for about 20 days before depositing it.

Growing Up

The cockroaches that are born alive stay with their mother for a day or so after coming into the world. Most baby cockroaches, however, are not born alive. Instead their mothers lay eggs that they hatch out of. As soon as they have hatched, they must take care of themselves. At first the babies are soft and white. But once exposed to the air, they soon harden and turn a darker color.

In the early part of their life, cockroaches are called **nymphs**. Although they look like adults, they are smaller and do not have reproductive organs or wings. Each time a nymph needs to grow, it has to shed its skin. Before becoming an adult, a cockroach can shed its skin between 5 and 14 times. The German cockroach takes about 95 days to become an adult and sheds its skin about six times. The American cockroach takes about 225 days. Depending on the species and the conditions, adult cockroaches can live for as little as a month or for several years.

It's not easy to spot the difference between a nymph and an adult cockroach. The nymph is at the top, and the adult is below.

A cockroach is attracted by the scent of a pitcher plant. Little does it know that this plant eats insects!

Antennas

When you see a cockroach moving its antennas, it is not waving to its friends—it is sniffing the air. In fact, cockroaches use their antennas as a nose. As cockroaches grow, their antennas get longer, and each time they shed a skin, new segments on their feelers appear. Cockroaches can also smell with their mouth. That is handy for sniffing out food.

A cockroach's sense of smell is very good. Among other things, it allows the roach to recognize members of its family. It also allows male cockroaches to find females who want a mate. When a female wants a partner, she releases a smelly chemical signal. The males hone in on her by following her scent as it wafts through the air.

In Touch

Cockroaches are very sensitive to movement.
That means it is quite hard to sneak up on
them from behind. One of the ways a cockroach
senses movements around it is through two
tiny hairs at the tip of its abdomen. These
hairs, called **cerci** (SUR-SI), pick up the smallest
movement or vibration in the air. Even a tiny
breeze caused by something small moving
nearby tells the cockroach that something is
happening. If the movement frightens the
cockroach, it will zoom off in the opposite
direction of whatever the cerci have detected.
Hairs that cover a cockroach's legs are also very
sensitive. They give a cockroach the important
sense of touch.

The cockroach has hairs on its legs for touch and hairs on its rear for feeling the air around it.

Smile please!
A close-up of a
giant cockroach
shows its two large
compound eyes.

Eye and Brain

A cockroach has a very different view of the world from a human's. Cockroaches have what are called "**compound eyes**." A human eye has just one lens, which focuses light rays entering the eye. But a cockroach eye is made up of as many as 2,000 separate lenses. A cockroach's eye cannot see as much detail as a human eye, although it can detect movement quite well. If cockroaches could drive, they would have problems at stoplights. That is because the cockroach's eye is not able to see the color red, but it is very sensitive to green light.

A cockroach's brain is much simpler than a human brain. Part of it is spread throughout the cockroach's body. In fact, there is a section of brain for each pair of legs!

Starve 'Em Out

Cockroaches can be serious pests. People are always looking for ways to kill them or drive them away. A good way to keep them away is to deprive them of food and water.

Cockroaches will eat anything that people eat. They also eat a lot of the things people might throw away or drop. So after every meal you eat, it is a good idea to sweep the floor and wash the dishes in hot, soapy water to get rid of all traces of grease. Be careful not to spread crumbs from room to room—eat in one room only and clean up afterward. Garbage should be put in a trash can that has a tight-fitting lid. Cookies, cereals, sugar, rice, and other possible snacks for cockroaches should be stored in sealed jars or plastic containers. If you have a pet cat or dog, clean its bowl after it has eaten and remove any food from the floor.

Cockroaches can't live long without water, so don't leave faucets dripping. Empty sinks after use and make sure that houseplants are not overwatered.

An American cockroach enjoys a tasty meal of cookies.

37

A cockroach feeds
on poisoned bait
put down by a
professional pest
controller.

No Hiding Place

Cockroaches love to find little nooks and crannies to live in. Once they have settled in, they will quickly spread throughout a building. To keep away these unwelcome guests, remove any places that could make a comfortable home for a cockroach. Garbage should be taken out as quickly as possible. Old cans or newspapers should not be kept for too long.

To stop cockroaches from spreading, fill in the holes around pipes. To prevent them from crawling up into your sinks at night, keep the plugs in.

Backwoods Bug

Only a handful of cockroach species are pests. But these annoying creatures have given all cockroaches a bad reputation.

In fact, most cockroach species are not pests at all. Most go quietly about their business. They have lived in the same places for a very long time, far away from people. The common wood cockroach is the country cousin of the city-dwelling pest cockroaches. It lives in the northern parts of the world. It likes to lurk under logs and stones, where conditions are moist. It is an unusual cockroach because the males and females look very different—they were once thought to be different species. The male is up to 1 inch (2.5 cm) long and has wings that extend past its abdomen. The female is smaller and has shorter wings.

"I'm not a pest!" The mountain cockroach lives far away from people in the damp forests of South Africa.

41

These cockroaches like to announce their presence on the island of Madagascar—with a hiss.

Unusual Suspects

There are about 5,000 species of cockroaches. They live in a variety of different places and have a wide range of habits. For example, the Madeira cockroach lets off a terrible smell when it feels threatened. This big, slow-moving cockroach is thought to have come from Africa originally. Then there is the Madagascar hissing cockroach that lives close to riverbanks. As you might guess from its name, this cockroach makes a hissing sound. It is a large, wingless cockroach. The giant cave cockroach from the rain forests of Central America and the Caribbean likes to live in caves with bats. The young cockroaches burrow into the bats' droppings. The species lives outside caves, too, where it finds shelter in hollow logs and trees.

How Big?

If you see a cockroach, it will probably be one of the pest species that lurks in homes, restaurants, and factories. These pest species include the American cockroach, German cockroach, and oriental, or common, cockroach. The American cockroach is the largest of the pest species and can grow to 2 inches (5 cm) long. The oriental cockroach is a little more than 1 inch (2.5 cm) long, and the German cockroach is less than ½ inch (1.2 cm) long.

If you ever go to Colombia, in South America, you might meet the giants of the cockroach world. These enormous roaches can grow to almost 4 inches (10 cm) long and more than 1½ inches (4 cm) wide.

The largest pest cockroach of them all—the adult American cockroach.

Determined to survive—an American cockroach crawls along a wall, searching for food.

Tough Guys

We humans are in an ongoing battle against the cockroaches that infest our homes, eat our food, and wander into restaurant kitchens for a free meal. But roaches show no signs of disappearing. That is hardly surprising because cockroaches have managed to survive for a very long time. Scientists think that cockroaches and their **ancestors** have been scuttling across Earth for at least 280 million years, possibly 320 million years. That means that they have outlived the dinosaurs.

Some scientists believe that cockroaches could outlive the human race, too. They think that if there was a nuclear war, cockroaches would survive much better than humans. In the rubble of a city hit by a nuclear missile, some of the first sounds to be made by living things could be those of cockroaches as they scavenge for food.

Robot Roach

Many scientists are fascinated by cockroaches. These strong, simple creatures have survived for millions of years. They have changed little in this time because they are so good at adapting to different conditions. By studying the growth and development of cockroaches, humans have discovered how amazing their bodies are. Some scientists even hope to create tiny moving machines by understanding how these insects' bodies work. They plan to base their machines on nature's clever designs. The machines would be like robotic roaches. They could perhaps be equipped with tiny television cameras and sent to search for landmines or even hunt inside collapsed buildings for earthquake survivors. We may think of cockroaches as a household pest, but they have inspired technology that may one day save many human lives!

Words to Know

Abdomen
: The rear part of an insect's body that contains the stomach and parts used to lay eggs.

Adapted
: Became better suited to a habitat or lifestyle.

Ancestors
: Early types of existing species.

Antennas
: Feelers on top of an insect's head that are used for smelling, touching, and tasting.

Cerci
: Tiny hairs at the back of a cockroach's body that detect movements in the air.

Chitin
: A substance in the skeleton of a cockroach.

Compound eyes
: Large eyes found on many insects. Each eye is made up of many parts.

Crop
: Section of the esophagus where food is stored.

Digest
: To break down food.

Esophagus
: The tube that leads from the mouth to the stomach.

Fat body	A cockroach's energy store and a place where chemicals dangerous to a cockroach are made safe.
Gizzard	The section inside a cockroach's body that is used to grind up food.
Habitat	The type of place where an animal or plant lives.
Insecticides	Chemicals that can kill insects.
Midgut	The section inside a cockroach's body that is used to absorb food into the blood.
Nymphs	Young cockroaches.
Salivary glands	Glands that make saliva, or spit.
Spiracles	Tiny holes in an insect's body case for taking in air.
Thorax	The middle part of an insect's body to which the wings and legs are attached.
Species	The scientific word for animals of the same kind that breed together.

Find Out More

Books

Green, E. K. *Cockroaches: World of Insects*. Blastoff!
Readers. Minnetonka, Minnesota: Bellwether Media,
2006.

Pyres, G. *Cockroaches Up Close*. Minibeasts Up Close.
Chicago, Illinois: Raintree, 2005.

Web sites

Madagascar Hissing Cockroach
animals.nationalgeographic.com/animals/wallpaper/
madagascar-hissing-cockroa_image.html
Download a picture of the Madagascar hissing cockroach.

PestWorld for Kids
www.pestworldforkids.org/cockroaches.html
Pictures and information about cockroaches.

Index